STRANGER
⊶FILLINGS⊷

STRANGER FILLINGS

THE MUFFIN BROTHERS

Running Press

PHILADELPHIA

Running Press
Hachette Book Group
1290 Avenue of the Americas, New York, NY 10104
www.runningpress.com
@Running_Press

Printed in China
Originally published in 2017 by the Orion Publishing Group, a division of Hachette UK
First U.S. Edition: October 2017

Published by Running Press, an imprint of Perseus Books, LLC, a subsidiary of Hachette Book Group, Inc.
The Hachette Speakers Bureau provides a wide range of authors for speaking events. To find out more, go to www.hachettespeakersbureau.com or call (866) 376-6591.
The publisher is not responsible for websites (or their content) that are not owned by the publisher.

Cover Design by the Muffin Brothers

Library of Congress Control Number: 2017944491
ISBNs: 978-0-7624-9056-1 (hardcover), 978-0-7624-9055-4 (ebook)

1010
10 9 8 7 6 5 4 3 2 1

TO DAD—
ONLY IN PASSING

CONTENTS

INTRODUCTION 1

WHAT YOU WILL NEED 2

DIFFICULTY 4

DEMOGORGON-ZOLA TARTLETS 8

D&D DELIGHTS 12

HOPPER'S COFFEE & CONTEMPLATION 16

BENNY'S BURGER 22

BARB'S MYSTERY DIP 26

LIGHT BITES 30

BAKED BRENNERS 36

EL'S COLA CRUSH 40

JOYCE'S CLOSE CALL 45

WILL'S FAKE CAKE 56

CAKE BYERS 60

JANE IVES'S DELICIOUS DIVE 64

EL'S TELEPATHIC Tart   72

FRIENDSHIP BITES   76

EL FLOTANTE   80

MONSTER HUNTING MEDLEY   86

ELEVEN'S EGGOS   90

MIKE'S ROCK CAKE RESCUE   95

FRIENDS DON'T LI(M)E PIE   102

THE UPSIDE DOWN CAKE   106

WILL'S SLUG SURPRISE   112

AUTHOR'S NOTE   118

WITH THANKS TO...   119

ABOUT THE AUTHORS   120

INTRODUCTION

There is another world.

A world where the trees look like spoons. Where the rivers run red with jam and the sky is darkened in a blizzard of sugar.

In 1984, two brothers made their way into this alternate, deliciously doughy netherworld.

This is their story...

Stranger Fillings

WHAT YOU WILL NEED

Do you know the difference between a slingshot and a wrist rocket?

Here are some essential items you will need on your quest.

DIFFICULTY

When you're about to embark on a ten-hour campaign into the Vale of Shadows you'd better know what you're doing.

Use this symbol to gauge the level of difficulty of each recipe:

EASY
"Mouth-breather"

MEDIUM
"Sometimes your total obliviousness just blows my mind"

HARD
"You're stealthy, like a ninja!"

DEMOGORGON-ZOLA

TARTLETS

"**Today we make contact**" with this monster of a snack

INGREDIENTS

FOR THE TARTLETS
1 sheet of ready-to-bake puff pastry dough
5 ounces blue cheese (we like Danish Blue, a vegetarian brand)
4 figs
Salt and pepper to taste

TO DECORATE
2 to 4 black olives
4 to 6 pine nuts

You will need: A cookie cutter in the shape of a man
   or a sharp knife

FEEDS

DIRECTIONS

Clear the work surface of any spilled blood before beginning. Pre-heat oven to 400ºF.

Roll out the puff pastry dough and use the pastry cutter to make a rough outline of the Demogorgon's body. Remove the head. Use excess strips of dough to fashion claws on the hands and feet. Repeat for a total of four pastries. Crumble the Gorgonzola over the pastries and use a knife to spread it evenly.

Bake the tarts in the oven for 20 minutes until golden.

Meanwhile, use a sharp knife to trim the tip of each fig and score into quarters without cutting all the way through. Open the figs up to make the Demogorgon's flower-shaped head. Use a knife to cut black olives into slices and place a slice in the center of each fig head. Cut the pine nuts into small, jagged pieces and place on top of the olives as shown.

Remove the tarts from the oven, let cool, and arrange each with a fig head.

Enjoy. Just be aware that as you soon as you touch this dish, things are going to get very bad, very quickly.

D&D DELIGHTS

Roll the dice with this deliciously retro recipe

INGREDIENTS

FOR THE COOKIES
4 cups all-purpose flour
4 egg yolks
2¾ cups (5½ sticks) firm butter
2 teaspoons vanilla extract or essence

TO DECORATE
1½ cups confectioners' sugar
2 egg whites
Black, white, and red food coloring

FOR THE COUNTER
2¾ ounces milk chocolate
Milk chocolate buttons
Flaked almonds
Sprinkles

You will need:
Hexagon-shaped cookie cutter or a sharp knife
Piping bag with a small round nozzle

FEEDS

DIRECTIONS

TO MAKE THE COOKIES

Put the flour in a bowl. Cut the butter into small pieces and add to the flour, and then rub the butter into the flour with your finger-tips until the mix looks like breadcrumbs. Add the sugar, egg yolks, and vanilla extract or essence, and mix to form a cookie dough. Put into a plastic bag and chill for at least 30 minutes.

Roll out the dough on a lightly floured surface to about 5mm thickness. Cut out hexagonal shapes with the cookie cutter or a knife and place them on a baking tray lined with baking parchment. Put back into the fridge to chill again for 30 minutes.

Preheat the oven to 350ºF. Bake the cookies for 12 to 15 minutes. Remove from oven and allow to cool on the tray before carefully lifting them off.

TO MAKE THE ICING

Sieve the confectioners' sugar into a small bowl, and add the egg white, little by little, beating well until a piping consistency is reached. With a piping bag fitted with a small plain nozzle (or small paper piping bag with the end cut off), pipe the outline sections of the dice on the individual cookies. If needed, loosen the texture of the icing with a little water. Divide the remainder into thirds, and color each a different shade of red (using the black food coloring to modify), as shown. Carefully fill the jacket shapes using a small teaspoon. Once completely dried, use a paintbrush to apply the white food coloring numbers.

TO MAKE THE COUNTER

Place the chocolate in a heatproof bowl, and set over a pan of simmering water, stirring occasionally just until melted. Use a piping bag with a small nozzle to pipe the shape on to baking parchment as shown. Insert the almonds and sprinkles as shown and leave in the freezer to cool. Use a little melted chocolate to affix the counter to a chocolate button as a base.

Your quest is over. If you are looking for a new challenge why not try to fashion a Thessalhydra?

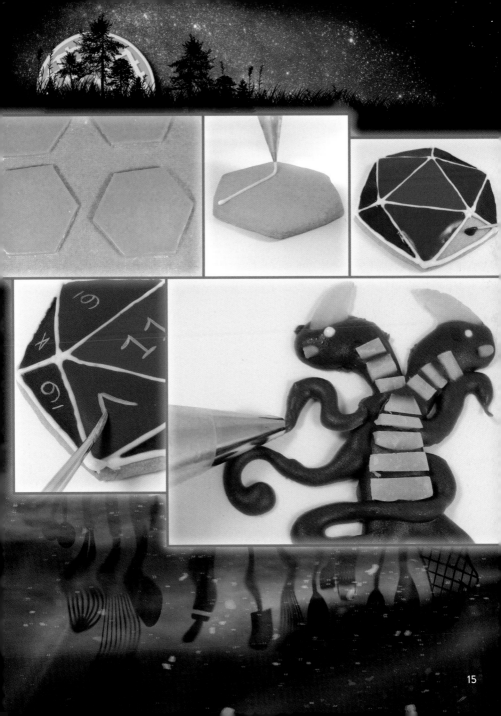

HOPPER'S COFFEE

& CONTEMPLATION

DIFFICULTY

With a hint of caffeine and alcohol, this is a dish to remember, with booze to help you forget

INGREDIENTS

FOR THE CUPCAKES
7 tablespoons soft butter
¾ cup superfine sugar
2 medium eggs, lightly beaten
¾ cup all-purpose flour
Just under 2 teaspoons baking powder
1 teaspoon coffee liqueur (just enough to kick-start your day)

FOR THE BUTTERCREAM
½ cup and 1 tablespoon (1 stick and 1 tablespoon) soft butter
2 cups confectioners' sugar
1 to 2 tablespoons
Pink food coloring

TO DECORATE
1 packet white chocolate buttons
1 Half-covered chocolate cookie
2 ounces milk chocolate
1 ounce white chocolate
Chocolate twigs
Chocolate sprinkles
Red sugar pearls
Black and red food coloring
Blue hard-shelled candy (i.e. M&M's)
Yellow chocolate star (you are the chief, after all!)

You will need:
A Muffin tin and 6 paper liners

FEEDS

DIRECTIONS

Get off the couch, brush your teeth, have a smoke and a swig of beer, and get on with it.
Preheat the oven to 350ºF. Place 6 liners into a muffin pan.

TO MAKE THE CUPCAKES
Put all the cupcake ingredients into a mixing bowl and beat well together, first with a wooden spoon, then with a whisk until properly mixed and smooth. With an ice cream scoop or a large spoon, divide the mix among the paper wrappers and bake for 15 to 20 minutes until the tops are golden. Transfer to a rack to cool completely before decorating.

TO MAKE THE FROSTING
Beat the confectioners' sugar and butter together in a freestanding electric mixer with a paddle attachment on medium-slow speed until they come together and are well mixed. Turn the mixer up to a medium-high speed and continue beating for at least 5 minutes until light and fluffy. Add a little of the pink food coloring and mix well with a teaspoon until the desired color is reached. Spoon or pipe the icing on top of the cold cakes. Store in the fridge to cool.

TO CREATE THE HAT
Use a knife to carve one of the spare cupcakes into the mound of the hat. Place the shaped cake on top of a half-covered chocolate cookie. Meanwhile, melt the milk chocolate very gently over hot water. Then use a knife to coat the cupcake and the biscuit so they fuse together. Place in the fridge to cool.

FOR THE FINISHING TOUCHES
Use a sharp knife to cut sticks out of the chocolate bar to make the eyebrows, and cut the white chocolate buttons to make the eyes. Use a paintbrush to apply the black and red food coloring to paint the eyes as shown. To make the cigarette, cut a length of chocolate bar and apply melted white chocolate (made with the above technique) and the red sugar pearls to form the lit end. Take the cupcake out of the fridge and draw a line to form the mouth, using a paintbrush and the black food coloring. Using a moistened toothpick, apply the chocolate sprinkles to create the beard, and then insert the cigarette. Add the eyes and eyebrows and the hat from the fridge. Affix the yellow chocolate star to the blue hard-shelled candy and fasten it to the cupcake sleeve with dabs of melted chocolate.

Stand back and admire your work. And if all else fails, throw a punch.

BENNY'S BURGER

Remember, if you want some food then you've got to talk first

INGREDIENTS

FOR THE LETTUCE
1 packet lime Jell-O

FOR THE BUN
2 tablespoons butter, softened
3 tablespoons superfine sugar
1 medium egg
3 tablespoons all-purpose flour
A pinch of baking powder
Sesame seeds

FOR THE REST OF THE BURGER
Half-covered chocolate cookies
2 ounces dark chocolate
Yellow-colored chewy fruit candies
Red piping gel
Edible paper
Red and blue food coloring

FEEDS

23

DIRECTIONS

TO MAKE THE LETTUCE

Follow the instructions on the packet of Jell-O, pour a thin layer into a shallow baking tray and set aside to cool.

TO MAKE THE BUN

Preheat the oven to 350°F. Line a muffin pan with paper wrappers. Put all the cake ingredients (using only half an egg) into a bowl and beat with a handheld electric mixer or wooden spoon until light and fluffy. Divide the mixture into the muffin cases. Bake for 10 to 15 minutes or until well risen, golden brown, and firm to the touch. Allow to cool for a couple of minutes, then transfer the cupcakes to a wire rack to cool completely. Use a knife to slice the top off both cupcakes. These will form the top and bottom buns of the burger. With a little vegetable oil and a toothpick, apply the sesame seeds to the top bun.

TO MAKE THE PATTY

Melt the chocolate in a bowl suspended over a pan of simmering water (do not allow the bottom of the bowl to touch the water). Then use a knife to cover the half-covered chocolate cookie in the melted chocolate. Set aside on a rack to cool. Once cooled, place it on the burger bun.

TO MAKE THE CHEESE

Place the chewy fruit candy on a microwaveable plate and microwave for 1 minute or until melted. Remove from the microwave and, once cool enough to handle, tease the candy into the shape of the cheese and add to the burger.

FOR THE FINISHING TOUCHES

Once the Jell-O has cooled, cut a lettuce-shaped section from the baking tray and add to the burger. Use the red piping gel to create a tomato sauce effect. With scissors, trim a flag from the edible paper and decorate using a paintbrush to apply the food coloring. Finally, use a sharp knife to cut a hole in the shape of a bullet wound into the top bun, and add the red food coloring for a suitably bloody effect using a fine paintbrush (as shown).

Check that any guests who show up sound the same as they did on the phone; otherwise . . .

BARB'S MYSTERY DIP

Easily overlooked, this sweet side-dish will be sorely missed once it's gone

INGREDIENTS

Gelatin, enough for about 5 cups water
1 package vanilla wafers
Licorice tubes
Licorice strings
Edible silver food color spray
A handful of clear hard candy or rock candy
Blue, red, and orange food coloring
4 ounces white chocolate

FEEDS

DIRECTIONS

TO MAKE THE POOL AND DIVING BOARD

Prepare the gelatin with water as directed on the packet. Put it in the fridge to speed up cooling, but don't let it set. Try not to think about Nancy and Jonathan. Once cooled, pour the gelatin liquid into your chosen bowl or cup and add blue food coloring until the desired shade is achieved.

Use a knife to cut the wafers into the shape of a diving board; you may need to stack 2 or 3 together to achieve the required strength. Be careful not to cut your hand. That would be a big mistake right now.

Melt 1 ounce of the white chocolate very gently over hot water. Using a knife, apply the chocolate to join the wafers together. Spray two strips of licorice with the edible silver food color spray and adhere them to the wafers with a bit more chocolate to form the rails. Use a small piece of licorice tube to form the underside of the diving board and seal the wafers to the rim of the gelatin bowl or cup. Hold in place until the chocolate cools and can support the diving board structure. (It's important to chill, Barb!)

TO MAKE THE GLASSES

Add the orange food coloring to the remaining white chocolate, place in the piping bag, and pipe the glasses' shape onto some nonstick baking paper.

Crush the clear hard candy to make flat shards. Use a toothpick to insert them into the frames of the glasses, before the chocolate cools.

FOR THE FINISHING TOUCHES

Finally, add just a touch of the red food coloring to the gelatin. Sit quietly and wait for the lights to go down. . . . It's dinner time!

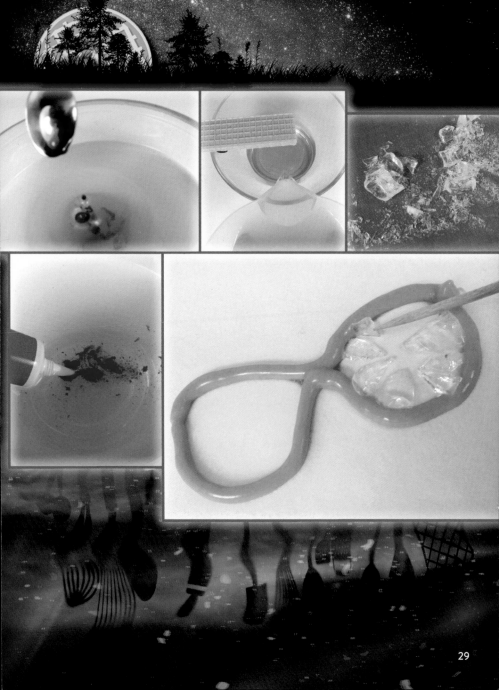

LIGHT BITES

DIFFICULTY

There's nothing like this electrifying trio of cupcakes to bring family back together

Ingredients

FOR THE CUPCAKES
7 tablespoons butter, softened
3/4 cup superfine sugar
2 medium eggs, lightly beaten
1 cup all-purpose flour
3 teaspoons baking powder

FOR THE BUTTERCREAM FROSTING
1/2 cup and 1 tablespoon (1 stick and 1 tablespoon) soft butter
2 cups confectioners' sugar

TO DECORATE
3 packs of hard-shelled candies (i.e. Peanut M&M's)
2 ounces milk chocolate

You will need:
Large piping bag with medium-sized star-shaped nozzle
Small piping bag with a small cone-shaped nozzle
Around 100 table lamps scattered around your house).

FEEDS

Directions

Get out the Christmas box from the attic.

TO MAKE THE CUPCAKES

Preheat the oven to 350ºF. Place 6 large paper wrappers into a muffin tin. Put all the cupcake ingredients into a mixing bowl and beat well together, first with a wooden spoon, then with a whisk until properly mixed and smooth. With an ice cream scoop or a large spoon, divide the mix evenly among the paper wrappers and bake for 15 to 20 minutes until the tops are golden. Transfer to a rack to cool completely before decorating.

TO MAKE THE FROSTING

Beat the confectioners' sugar and butter together in a freestanding electric mixer with a paddle attachment on medium-slow speed until they come together and are well mixed. Turn the mixer up to a medium-high speed and continue beating for at least 5 minutes until light and fluffy.

Use the large piping bag with the star-shaped nozzle to pipe the buttercream frosting onto the cupcakes in a swirl pattern. Melt the milk chocolate very gently over hot water and, once melted, use the small piping bag and nozzle to create the wiring for the lights. Apply a selection of the hard-shelled candies to form the pattern of lights along the chocolate wiring.

Stand back and watch the light show. Remember, one blink for "yes" and two for "no."

BAKED

BRENNERS

Once you Papa you can't stop!

INGREDIENTS

FOR THE COOKIES
4 cups all-purpose flour
1¾ cups (3½ sticks) firm butter
1½ cups confectioners' sugar
Yolks of 4 medium eggs
2 teaspoons vanilla extract or essence

TO DECORATE
1½ cups confectioners' sugar
Whites of 2 medium eggs
Black food coloring
1½ cups superfine sugar
1 medium egg white
¼ teaspoon cream of tartar
Pinch of salt
2 teaspoons vanilla extract or essence

You will need:
Gingerbread man cookie cutter or sharp knife
A piping bag with nozzle but no parenting skills whatsoever

FEEDS

DIRECTIONS

TO MAKE THE COOKIES

Put the flour in a bowl. Cut the butter into small pieces and add to the flour. Then rub the butter into the flour with your fingertips until the mix looks like breadcrumbs. Add the sugar, egg yolks, and vanilla extract or essence, and mix to form a cookie dough. Put into a plastic bag and chill for at least 30 minutes.

Roll out the dough on a lightly floured surface to about 5mm thickness. Cut out Brenner shapes with a cookie cutter or knife (feel free to readjust his arms as pictured) and place them on a baking tray lined with baking parchment. Put back into the fridge to chill again for 30 minutes.

Preheat the oven to 350°F. Bake the cookies for 12 to 15 minutes. Remove from oven and allow to cool on the tray before carefully lifting them off.

TO MAKE THE FROSTING

Sieve the confectioners' sugar into a small bowl, and add the egg white, little by little, beating well until a piping consistency is reached. Divide into two quantities—one twice as big as the other—and use the black food coloring to color the larger set dark gray and the smaller set light gray. With a piping bag fitted with a small plain nozzle (or a small paper piping bag with the end cut off), pipe the outline of the jacket and shirt. Loosen the texture of the light gray icing with a little water if needed, then carefully fill the jacket shape using a small teaspoon and a toothpick. Allow to set.

Ask your daughter to kill a cat and watch as she fails. You're not angry. You're just disappointed.

TO MAKE THE MERINGUE HAIR

Whisk the sugar, egg whites, cream of tartar, salt, and $\frac{1}{3}$ cup of water in a heatproof bowl. Put the bowl over a saucepan of simmering water and whisk with a handheld electric mixer on low speed, then gradually increase the speed to high and beat until soft peaks form. This will take 5 to 10 minutes.

Remove the bowl from the saucepan and continue beating until the meringue is cool and fluffy. Add the vanilla. With a piping bag fitted with a star nozzle, pipe on the meringue mix to create the hair.

Take pride in the fact that your "daughter" has the power to kill people with her mind.

EL'S COLA CRUSH

Test your powers of concentration with some experimental eating

INGREDIENTS

FOR THE CUPCAKES
1 egg
½ cup milk
4 tablespoons vegetable oil
1 2/3 cups all-purpose flour
¾ cup superfine sugar
2 teaspoons baking powder
½ teaspoon salt

FOR THE BUTTERCREAM
½ cup (1 stick) soft butter
2 cups confectioners' sugar
1 to 2 tablespoons milk
Pink food coloring

TO DECORATE
Strawberry licorice strings
Chocolate sprinkles
Mini marshmallows
Licorice strings
1 pack white chocolate buttons
White food coloring
Rice paper
Edible silver food color spray

You will need:
White cupcake liners
A camcorder to record any
    unusual activity

FEEDS

DIRECTIONS

Focus.

TO MAKE THE COKE CAN

Follow the instructions on the packet to prepare the Jell-O and set aside to cool. Crumple one of the plastic cups, taking care not to split it, and use an elastic band to hold it in place. Pour in the cooled Jell-O and leave in the fridge to set.

TO MAKE THE CUPCAKES

Preheat the oven to 400°F and line a muffin pan with 6 paper wrappers.

Beat the egg with a fork. Then stir in the milk and oil. Sift flour into a large bowl. Add sugar, baking powder, and salt. Add the egg mixture to the flour and stir until the flour is moistened. The batter should be lumpy. Do not overmix.

Fill the muffin wrappers two-thirds full. Bake for 20 to 25 minutes or until golden brown. Once cooked, tip the muffins out onto a rack and leave to cool completely.

TO MAKE THE BUTTERCREAM

Beat the butter in a large bowl until soft. Gently add half the confectioners' sugar and beat until smooth Add the remaining confectioners' sugar with a little milk, adding more as necessary to make a light fluffy icing. Add the pink food coloring little by little and mix until well combined. Really, really focus.

Use a knife to apply the buttercream. Add chocolate sprinkles to create the hairline. Use a sharp knife to cut the licorice into short strands and affix to the buttercream. Use a paintbrush to apply white food coloring to the strawberry licorice laces and thread the laces through the mini marshmallows. Using a fine paintbrush, apply the black food coloring to the white chocolate buttons to create the slits of the eyes and pupils. Next, apply the purple food coloring to color the eyelids. Use a little melted chocolate to affix the decorated buttons to the face of the cupcake.

TO CREATE THE LID AND RING-PULL FOR THE COKE CAN

Use a sharp knife to cut a shape from the rice paper and color it with the food spray. Once the Jell-O is set, apply the lid. Melt the white chocolate buttons very gently over hot water. Once melted, use a small piping bag and nozzle to apply decoration to the can's exterior.

It's over! As unpleasant as that might have been, it's not like you would ever be forced to kill a cat or anything horrific like tha– . . . Oh.

STRANGER FILLINGS

PLAYER'S MANUAL

FANTASY ROLE PLAYING GAME

JOYCE'S CLOSE CALL

The original dine and dash, these treats spell danger

INGREDIENTS

FOR THE COOKIES
2¼ cups all-purpose flour
1⅔ sticks firm butter
¾ cup confectioners' sugar
2 egg yolks
1 teaspoon vanilla extract or
  essence

FOR THE CAKE
1⅓ cups (2½ sticks) butter
2 cups sugar
6 eggs (lightly beaten)
3 cups all-purpose flour
6 teaspoons baking powder
¾ cup and 2½ tablespoons cocoa powder, sieved
3 to 4 tablespoons milk
1¼ cups soft butter
1 cup confectioners' sugar
1 to 2 tablespoons milk
Strawberry or raspberry jam

TO DECORATE
¾ cup confectioners' sugar
1 egg white
Red and black food coloring
1 packet chocolate peanut candies (i.e. Peanuts M&Ms)
1 packet Kit Kats
18 ounces fondant
1 packet chocolate twigs
Black and yellow food coloring

You will need:
A circular cookie cutter and ide-
  ally "R," "U," and "N" shaped
  cutters (though you can use a
  sharp knife instead)
A fine paintbrush

FEEDS

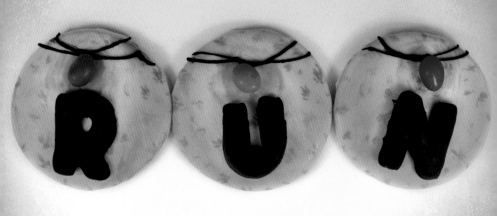

DIRECTIONS (continued)

TO MAKE THE COOKIES

Put the flour in a bowl. Cut the butter into small pieces and add to the flour. Then rub the butter into the flour with your fingertips until the mix looks like breadcrumbs. Add the sugar, egg yolks, and vanilla extract or essence, and mix to form a cookie dough. Put into a plastic bag and chill for at least 30 minutes.

Roll out the dough on a lightly floured surface to about 5mm thickness. Cut out shapes with the circular cutter, and use the cookie cutters or a knife to cut out the word "RUN." Place them on a baking tray lined with baking parchment. Put back into the fridge to chill again for 30 minutes.

Meanwhile, preheat the oven to 350°F. Bake the cookies for 12 to 15 minutes, until they begin to brown around the edges. (The letters will cook much more quickly than the cookies, so keep an eye on them.) Remove from the oven and allow to cool on the tray before carefully lifting off.

TO MAKE THE ICING

Sieve the confectioners' sugar into a small bowl, and add the egg white, little by little, beating well until a flooding consistency (should be thinner than piping consistency) is reached. Separate out roughly one quarter of the icing and add black food coloring to it. Use a wooden spoon to flood the letters as shown. Next, add the yellow food coloring to the remaining icing. Place the round cookies on a wire rack over a bowl or tray to catch the run-off, and use a spoon to flood the cookies with the icing until a smooth, even surface is achieved.

Use a paintbrush to add the black, yellow, and brown food coloring to make the wallpaper decoration. Use a small piping bag and nozzle to apply the black wiring to the biscuits and affix red, blue, and green peanut candies (i.e. Peanuts M&Ms) using a little leftover icing. Use a paintbrush to apply red, blue, and green food coloring as shown to create a faux glow. Lastly, use a bit of icing to affix the "R," "U," and "N" to the cookies beneath the lights.

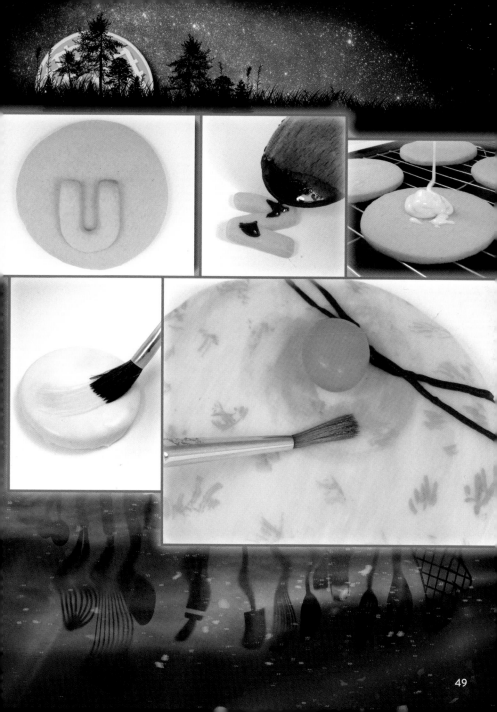

DIRECTIONS

TO MAKE THE CAKE

Preheat the oven to 325°F. Grease and line a 13 x 9-inch deep rectangular baking pan. Cream butter and sugar until pale in color, light, and fluffy. Add the eggs very gradually, beating well between each addition. Fold the flour into the mix until blended. Add enough milk to give a dropping consistency and spoon into the prepared pan, smoothing the top and making a slight dip in the center.

Bake for 45 to 55 minutes, or until firm to the touch and a knife inserted in the center comes out clean. Cool in the pan for a few minutes, then turn out onto a rack to cool completely.

TO MAKE THE BUTTERCREAM FROSTING

Beat the butter in a large bowl until soft. Gently add half the confectioners' sugar and beat until smooth Add the remaining confectioners' sugar with a little milk, adding more as necessary to make a light fluffy frosting.

FOR THE FINISHING TOUCHES

Use a knife to cut the cake in half, and then add buttercream frosting between the two halves along with the jam. Cut the Kit Kats to be the same height as the cake and use a little melted chocolate to affix them to the outside of the cake as paneling.

Shape the chocolate twigs in the form of a claw, using a little melted chocolate to hold them together. Once complete, use a paintbrush to decorate the claw with red and black food coloring and then insert into the top of the cake. Roll out almost all of the fondant, adding a little of the yellow food coloring as required, on a floured surface and then drape over the cake and claw, allowing the icing to tear and the claw to penetrate. Add yellow food coloring to the remaining fondant and fashion the telephone, as shown. Use the paintbrush to apply the black and yellow food coloring to create the wallpaper pattern.

Place the "RUN" cookies atop or alongside the cake.

Now get out of the house as quickly as you can and try not to think about how much it will cost to have the wallpaper redone.

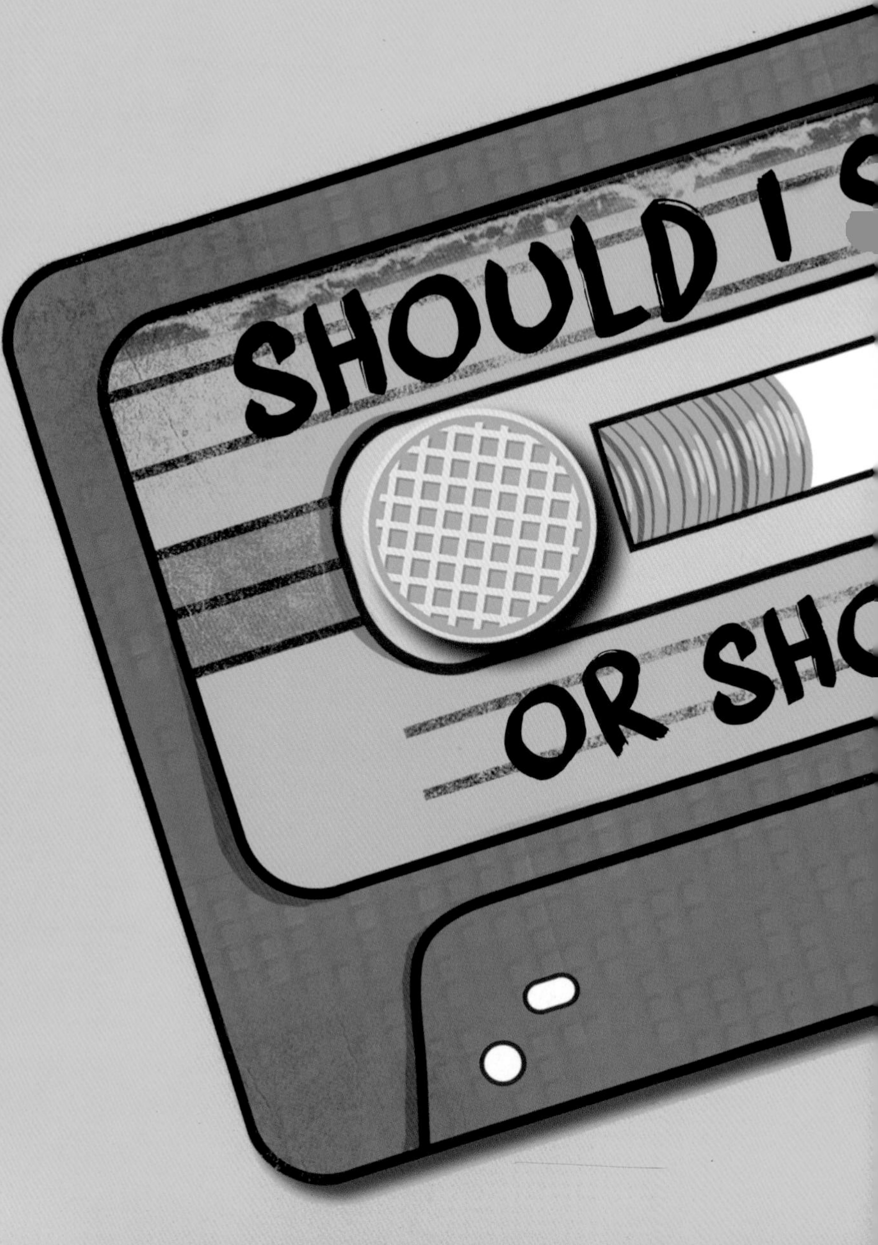
SHOULD I
OR

WILL'S FAKE CAKE

DIFFICULTY

A familiar face with a very surprising stuffing

Ingredients

FOR THE BRIOCHE BOY
7 tablespoons warm water
1 teaspoon dried yeast
2 tablespoons warm milk
1 tablespoon superfine sugar
2¼ cups strong bread flour (look for high-gluten flour), plus extra for dusting
½ teaspoon salt
2 tablespoons butter
1 large egg, lightly beaten
1 egg yolk (for glazing)

TO DECORATE
9 ounces milk chocolate
Black food coloring
Blue fondant
1 packet white marshmallows

You will need:
Piping bag and nozzle

FEEDS

DIRECTIONS

TO MAKE THE BRIOCHE BOY

Mix the warm water, yeast, warm milk, and sugar in a bowl. Let it stand for 5 minutes until it begins to froth up. Mix the flour and salt together in a large mixing bowl, and rub in the butter until the mixture resembles fine breadcrumbs. Make a well in the center and add the yeast mixture and the beaten egg.

Use your hands to knead into a very sticky dough, adding just enough flour to make it workable. Tip the dough out onto a floured work surface and knead well for 10 minutes until it feels a little elastic—it will still be very sticky at this stage, but don't be tempted to add too much flour. Place the dough into an oiled bowl, cover with cling film, and set aside to rise for 2 to 3 hours or until doubled in size.

Tip out onto the floured work surface and knead again for 2 minutes. The dough should be much less sticky now, but add a little flour if it needs it. Press the dough out into a rectangle roughly 10 x 6 inches. Using a sharp knife, cut out the shape of the boy, using a round cutter for the head, held at an angle so as not to sever it from his body at the neck.

Place him onto a greased baking sheet, cover lightly with oiled cling film, and leave for about 1 hour or until doubled in size again.

Preheat the oven to 400°F. Beat the egg yolk with a little water and brush it over the brioche shape. Bake for 20 to 30 minutes or until golden, then place on a rack to cool. Once cooled, flip over the brioche figure and get a sharp knife ready. Take a deep breath, because this next part is going to be unpleasant. Ready?

Cut out the back of the torso and remove some of the brioche. Insert as many marshmallows as you can before replacing the back and carefully turn the brioche figure over, keeping the back intact. Use the knife to cut a hole in the front of the figure and carefully tease out some of the marshmallows so they stick out.

TO MAKE THE HAIR

Melt the chocolate in a bowl suspended over a pan of simmering water (do not allow the bottom of the bowl to touch the water), allow it to cool a little, and then add it to the piping bag and nozzle. Begin piping the strands of hair. Use a paintbrush to apply the black food coloring for the eyes and mouth. Roll out the fondant—using flour both on the surface and on the rolling pin—and shape into the blanket as shown.

Tease out the stuffing with a mixture of relief and horror, as you realize those pesky kids might be on to something. . . .

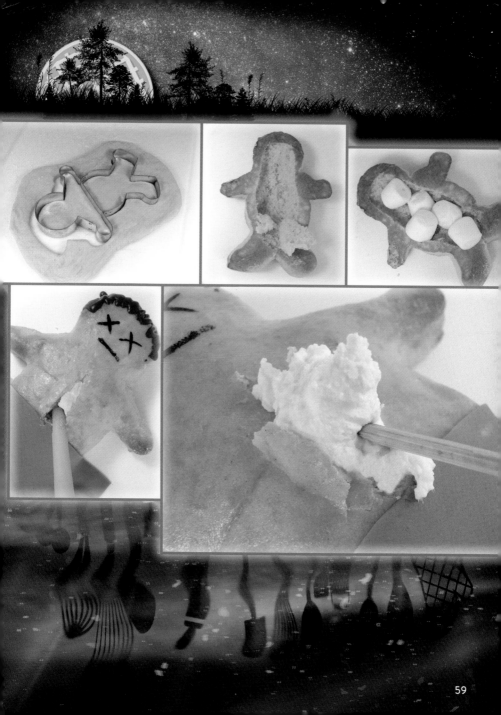

CAKE

BYERS

DIFFICULTY

Go to your special place with this delicious shack of a snack

INGREDIENTS

FOR THE CAKE
$1^1/_3$ cup soft butter
2 cups sugar
6 medium eggs, lightly beaten
$2^3/_4$ cups all-purpose flour
$2^3/_4$ teaspoons baking powder
$^3/_4$ cup and 2 tablespoons cocoa
   powder, sifted
$^1/_3$ cup milk

FOR THE BUTTERCREAM
$3^1/_2$ cups confectioners' sugar,
   sifted
1 cup (2 sticks) soft butter
1 to 2 tablespoons milk
Brown food coloring

FOR THE EDIBLE SOIL
$2^1/_2$ ounces plain cooking chocolate, chopped into pieces
$^3/_4$ cup superfine sugar
2 tablespoons water

TO DECORATE
1 packet chocolate twigs
1 package vanilla wafers
Rice paper
Brown, red, yellow, orange, and blue food
   coloring
$5^1/_3$ ounces milk chocolate
1 packet chocolate cream cookie
White chocolate stars

You will need:
Small piping bag with small plain nozzle

FEEDS

DIRECTIONS

Remember, you're not like other kids.

TO MAKE THE CAKE

Preheat the oven to 350ºF. Grease and line an 8-inch pie pan. Cream the butter and sugar until pale in color, light and fluffy. Add the eggs very gradually, beating well between each addition. Combine the flour and cocoa powder, then fold into the mix until blended. Add enough milk to give a dropping consistency and spoon into the prepared pan, smoothing the top and making a slight dip in the center.

Bake for 45 to 55 minutes, or until firm to the touch and a knife inserted in the center comes out clean. Cool in the pan for a few minutes, then turn out onto a rack to cool completely.

TO MAKE THE BUTTERCREAM

Beat the confectioners' sugar and butter together until light and fluffy, adding a little milk if necessary. Add the brown food coloring and stir until the correct color is achieved. Use a knife to spread the frosting in a thick, even layer on top of the cooled cake.

TO MAKE THE EDIBLE SOIL

Heat the sugar and water in a pan and insert a sugar thermometer. When the sugar reaches 266ºF, take it off the heat. If you don't have a thermometer, wait until all the sugar is dissolved and starting to change to a medium brown color. Add the chopped plain cooking chocolate and stir with a whisk. Make sure all the sugar coats the chocolate and stir for about 1 minute.

Empty out the mixture onto a piece of foil to cool. Spread the "soil" evenly onto the cake.

TO MAKE THE LEAVES

Use a paintbrush to apply the orange food coloring to the wafers. Leave to dry. Then use scissors to cut the now-colored wafers into small pieces before using your hands to crumble it into tiny pieces. Sprinkle some of this onto the edible soil.

TO MAKE THE TREE BRANCHES

Melt the chocolate very gently over hot water. Leave to cool for a few minutes before transferring to the piping bag. Pipe the tree shapes onto some baking parchment. Carefully add some of the crushed up "leaves." Then chill until firm.

Use a knife to smear some melted chocolate on the parchment paper to make the sign as shown. Construct the fort by placing the chocolate twigs into the cake as shown and using some of the melted chocolate to fix them together and affix the sign.

Remove the trees from the fridge and place them on top of the completed fort. Cut a sheet of edible paper and use the paintbrush to decorate with the food coloring and do the same to the chocolate signs. To make the tire, halve the chocolate cream cookie and use a circular cutter moistened with a little milk to slowly remove the center.

TO MAKE THE FLAG

Use a paintbrush to decorate the rice paper and then add the chocolate stars.

Mom is coming to get you, so just hold on and try not to eat too many slugs in the meantime.

JANE IVES'S
DELICIOUS DIVE

Let your mind wander with this submersible snack

INGREDIENTS

2 packets green Jell-O
Sour Spaghetti (or Cola Laces if you can find them)
Yellow food color spray
2 tablespoons butter
6 ounces mini marshmallows
3 ounces crisped rice cereal (i.e. Rice Krispies)
10 ounces white chocolate, divided
3 ounces dark chocolate
Brown or caramel food coloring

You will need:
A tube-shaped glass or jar
A small can
A cake pop stick

FEEDS

DIRECTIONS

FOR JANE IVES

Grease a 13 x 9-inch baking pan. Melt the butter in a large, heavy-based saucepan over low heat. Add the marshmallows and cook gently until they are completely melted and blended, stirring constantly. Mix well. Take the pan off the heat and immediately add the cereal, mixing lightly until well coated. Let the mix cool before shaping it into a head and a body. It will be very sticky, so wet your hands if necessary. Insert the cake pop stick into the head and leave the head and body separate for now.

FOR THE WHITE CHOCOLATE COATING

Place 7 ounces of the white chocolate in a heatproof bowl and set over a pan of simmering water, stirring occasionally until just melted. Remove from the heat and add the brown or caramel food coloring.

TO CREATE THE HAND

Pipe a bit of the melted white chocolate onto some baking parchment in the shape of a hand and leave to cool just long enough to harden slightly. Remove it from the parchment and use a toothpick to stick it to the inside of your jar, then place the jar in the fridge.

TO COMPLETE JANE IVES

Dip the head and body in the remaining melted colored chocolate to create an even covering and place in the fridge to cool. Once cooled, use a toothpick to apply first melted white chocolate and then dark chocolate to create the face as shown. Cut the remaining, un-melted white chocolate into four small rectangles and affix to the front of Jane's body.

TO CREATE JANE'S MASK

Wrap the soda can in baking parchment and use a knife to apply melted chocolate over the parchment. Once it has begun to cool, use the knife to cut the shape of the bottom of El's mask (as shown) and place it in the fridge. Once completely cooled, remove the bottom of the "mask" and affix to the head to the top and the body to the underside using a little melted chocolate and place the entire thing in the fridge to cool. After it has cooled, use the same dark chocolate that makes up the face to finish the details of the mask as shown.

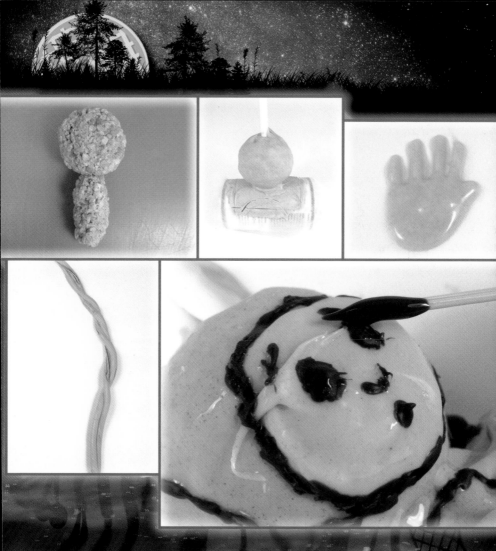

FOR THE FINISHING TOUCHES

Prepare the green Jell-O following the ingredients on the packet and pour into the jar that has the hand stuck to the inside. Put it the fridge to begin to set. To create the air tube, use the yellow food color spray to colour one of the Sour Spaghetti strings and use a little melted chocolate to affix it to the body. Place the figure in the jelly and leave to fully set in the fridge.

Wave goodbye to Papa as you sink in. Your world is about to turn upside down!

BAKE ON THROUGH TO THE OTHER SIDE!

EL'S TELEPATHIC TART

(WITH RUSSIAN DRESSING)

DIFFICULTY

A cold war classic—take a trip to the other side with these transporting treats

INGREDIENTS

FOR THE CAKE
¼ cup cocoa powder, plus extra for dusting
3 tablespoons boiling water
¾ cup superfine sugar
¾ cup and 2 tablespoons all-purpose flour
2 teaspoons baking powder
2 large eggs
½ cup margarine (reserve some for greasing)

FOR THE MOUSSE
11 ounces plain chocolate (no more than 40 to 50 percent cocoa solids), broken into squares
2 cups heavy cream

FOR THE FIGURES
White fondant
Pink, khaki or pale green, black, and blue food coloring
Chocolate sprinkles

FOR THE MIRROR GLAZE
2 tablespoons gelatin powder
⅓ cup cold water
1½ tablespoon water
1 cup sugar
⅔ cup glucose or corn syrup
½ cup sweetened, condensed milk
1¼ cup chocolate
Black food coloring gel

FEEDS

Directions

Head towards the guy with the funny hat.

TO MAKE THE CAKE

Preheat the oven to 350ºF. Grease a 13 x 9-inch pie or tart pan with margarine and line the base and sides with baking paper. You need to line the pan right to the top even though the cake will not fill it. Measure the cocoa powder into a large bowl. Pour in the boiling water and mix to a paste with a spatula. Add the rest of the dry ingredients, the eggs, and margarine, and beat until smooth using a handheld mixer. Spoon the cake mixture into the prepared pie or tart pan and level the surface with a palette knife.

Bake in the oven for 20 to 25 minutes, or until a skewer or knife inserted into the center of the cake comes out clean and the cake feels springy to the touch. (This would be easier if you had a basic grasp of Russian.)

TO MAKE THE MOUSSE

Place the chocolate in a bowl and melt over a pan of gently simmering water (do not allow the base of the bowl to touch the water). Stir continuously, taking care not to let the chocolate get too hot. Set aside to cool a little. Pour the cream into a separate bowl and whip it until soft peaks form when the whisk is removed. Carefully fold in the melted chocolate until smooth and not streaky.

When the cake has cooled, and while it is still in the pan, spoon the chocolate mousse on top and level with a palette knife. Cover the pan with cling film and chill in the fridge for a minimum of 4 hours (preferably overnight) until the mousse is firm.

TO MAKE THE MIRROR GLAZE

Bloom the gelatin in the cold water. Allow to sit. Separately, boil water, sugar, and glucose in a saucepan over medium heat until fully dissolved. Remove from heat and add in the gelatin. Add the condensed milk to the mixture. (Wait . . . what was that noise?) Pour the entire warm mixture over the chocolate in a bowl. Allow to sit for 5 minutes. Stir carefully. Use a thermometer to see when the temperature reaches 90ºF and is ready for pouring. Color the glaze with the gel food coloring.

FOR THE FINISHING TOUCHES

Cover a surface or rimmed baking sheet with cling wrap for easy cleanup. Pour the glaze over the cake and allow the excess run off. To finish, take a long offset (or icing) spatula and hold it perfectly level to the top. Swipe the spatula across the top, just barely above the cake level to remove any excess. This will leave your finish looking flat and perfect.

Allow the cake rest to set before moving it.

Roll out the fondant to create the figures. Use the chocolate
sprinkles to decorate the man's hat and use food coloring and a
small paintbrush to apply their features. Use toothpicks to place
them in the cake.

Scream with horror as the kitchen walls crumble and your guests
scramble for safety.

FRIENDSHIP BITES

Friends don't lie, but they sure do taste good

INGREDIENTS

FOR THE POPS
3½ tablespoons butter
1½ cup mini marshmallows
¾ cup crisped rice cereal (i.e. Rice Krispies)
4 ounces milk chocolate
4 ounces white chocolate
4 ounces red chocolate,
(All chocolate should be broken into pieces.)

TO DECORATE
Sour Spaghetti (or Cola laces if available)
Red, blue, and white fondant
Edible paper
Green and black food coloring
Petal paste

You will need:
3 cake pop sticks

FEEDS

LUCAS   MIKE   DUSTIN

Directions

TO MAKE THE CAKE POPS

Grease a 13 x 9-inch pan. Melt the butter in a large, heavy based saucepan over low heat. Add the marshmallows and cook gently until they are completely melted and blended, stirring constantly. Mix well. Take the pan off the heat and immediately add the cereal, mixing lightly until well coated. Let the mix cool before dividing into three equal portions and shaping each into a head. It will be very sticky, so wet your hands if necessary.

Once complete, use a sharp knife to cut the upper quarter from one of the heads. Set aside this offcut for later. Use a knife to make a small hole in the base of each of the heads. (Remember the rule: "if you draw first blood . . . ") Insert the cake pop sticks with a little melted chocolate. Place the three heads upright in a freezer to harden.

TO MAKE THE CHOCOLATE COATINGS

For the chocolate coatings, place the milk chocolate in a heat-proof bowl. Place white and red chocolates combined in a separate heatproof bowl. Set both over a pan of simmering water, stirring occasionally just until melted and mixing the red and white chocolate to make a pink. Don't let the water boil, unless you're a goblin with an intelligence score of zero.

FOR THE FINISHING TOUCHES

Remove both from the heat and use a palette knife to apply the chocolate to one of the heads and the white chocolate mixture to the other two. Using a fine paintbrush, apply the black food coloring to create the faces of Lucas, Mike, and Dustin. Set aside a little melted chocolate for decoration.

For Lucas's head, dip the top of the milk chocolate-covered head into a bowl of dark chocolate sprinkles. Use a knife to cut a strip from the edible paper and then using a paintbrush to apply the green and black food colors to make a camouflage pattern. When dry, wrap the paper around his head to make a bandana.

For Mike's head, use a small piping bag and nozzle to pipe the leftover milk chocolate to form the hair.

For Dustin's head, use a sharp knife to cut the Cola laces to length and, using a bit of melted chocolate, affix them to the head. Roll out the icing and use a sharp knife to cut the pattern for the cap and lay it on the offcut of the head prepared earlier. To make the peak of the cap you may need to use some petal paste to stiffen the icing. Attach to the head, on top of the hair, with melted chocolate.

Share and enjoy. And remember that you can have more than one best friend.

EL FLOTANTE

Harnessing the awesome power of jello, this powerful dish will heighten your senses

INGREDIENTS

FOR THE EL-SHAPED CAKE
$1/2$ cup all-purpose flour
1 teaspoon baking powder
$3^1/2$ tablespoons butter, at
   room temperature
$1/2$ cup superfine sugar
1 egg (not Eggo)

FOR THE POOL PARFAIT
Gelatin (enough for 5 cups of
   water)
Blue food coloring
Ladyfingers
2 ounces chocolate (white or
   milk)

TO DECORATE
$1^1/4$ cup crème anglaise (or vanilla
   pudding)
Pink food coloring
1 pack of mini marshmallows
Blue fondant (enough for the goggles as shown)

You will need:
A "water tank"-shaped receptacle
Gingerbread man—or even better,
   woman—cutter. (You may find this
   treat gets mistaken for being a
   boy though.)
Toothpicks
A piping bag and small nozzle
(It helps to have a crackly radio on
   the side.)

FEEDS

DIRECTIONS

Find an empty school and fill a small pool with room temperature water. Preheat the oven to 350ºF.

TO MAKE THE POOL PARFAIT

Prepare the gelatin as directed on the packet and add some blue food coloring. Put it in the fridge to speed up cooling, but don't let it set.

Warm some of the chocolate gently over a pan of warm water and use the melted chocolate to stick the Ladyfingers to the bottom of the water tank-shaped receptacle.

Pour the gelatin on top of the Ladyfingers and place the bowl in the fridge to set fully.

TO MAKE THE CAKE

Grease a 13 x 9-inch pan. Place the ingredients for the cake into a large bowl and mix together with a handheld electric mixer. Pour the mixture into the pan, place in the oven and bake for 15 to 20 minutes until golden brown. Cool on a wire rack. Once cooled, use the cookie cutter to cut out an El shape.

Apply the pink food coloring to the crème anglaise or pudding to turn it the desired shade of pink for the dress. Pour it on top of the cake figure and use a knife to spread it out evenly. Use a toothpick to apply the marshmallows as shown. Use a sharp knife to cut the goggles from the fondant, then apply to the cake. Finally, fill a piping bag with a little chocolate and pipe on the mouth.

Now it's time to go and see Will, so dive in!

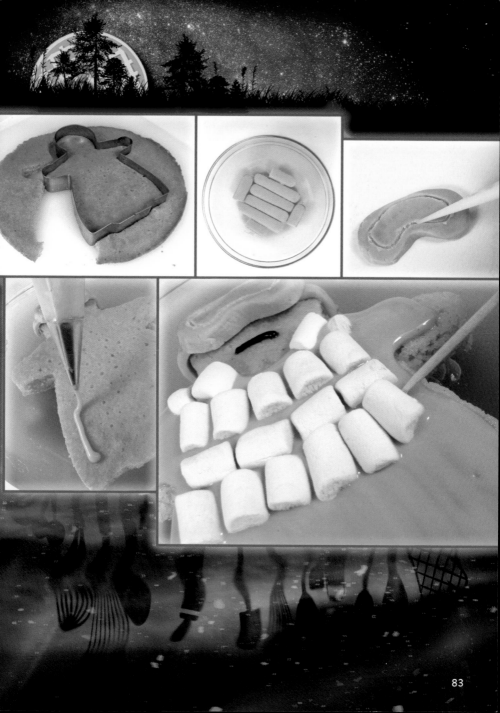

MONSTER–HUNTING MEDLEY

DIFFICULTY

Prepare for a bite-sized battle with these deadly delights

INGREDIENTS

FOR THE BASEBALL BAT
2 tablespoons butter
$^2/_3$ cup mini marshmallows
$^1/_3$ cup crisped rice cereal (e.g. Rice Krispies)
3 ounces milk chocolate
2 ounces dark chocolate
(Chocolate should be broken into pieces, like Steve and Nancy's relationship)
Silver food color spray

TO MAKE THE GAS CAN
Mallomar candy
3 ounces red candy melts
Sour Spaghetti (Cola laces if available)
Silver food color spray
Chocolate twigs

TO MAKE THE BEAR TRAP
Black fondant (if you're up to construction challenge), or
1 packet Kit Kat bars
Black food color spray
Red licorice strings

You may also need:
4 boxes of .38 caliber rounds

FEEDS

DIRECTIONS

TO MAKE THE BASEBALL BAT

Grease a 13 x 9-inch tray bake tin. Melt the butter in a large, heavy-based saucepan over low heat. Add the marshmallows and cook gently until they are completely melted and blended, stirring constantly. Mix well. Take the pan off the heat and immediately add the cereal, mixing lightly until well coated. Let the mix cool before shaping it into a bat as shown. It will be very sticky, so wet hands if necessary.

Place the two different chocolates in separate heatproof bowls and set them over a pan of simmering water, stirring occasionally just until melted. Remove from the heat and use a palette knife to apply to the exterior of the bat: first the milk chocolate, and then brush the darker chocolate on top to create streaks and decoration. Use a sharp knife to cut the chocolate twigs into "nails" and spray them silver with the edible spray. Use a little melted chocolate to fix them to the bat. Leave somewhere cool to harden.

TO MAKE THE GAS CAN

Place the red candy melts in a heatproof bowl and set over a pan of simmering water, stirring occasionally just until melted. Remove from the heat and use a palette knife to apply to the exterior of the Mallomar. Use a knife to cut a chocolate twig into the shape of the nozzle and decorate with melted red candy and a loop of Cola lace decorated with silver food spray.

TO MAKE THE BEAR TRAP

Use a sharp knife to cut the Kit Kat bars, shape into a square and handle as shown, and join together with extra melted red candy from the gas can. Apply the black food spray, and after it sets, weave the red licorice strings throughout as shown in the lower picture. If you're up to a challenge, use black fondant to craft the detailed version shown in the upper picture.

For best results, begin with the baseball bat, then move on to the trap, before finishing things off with the gas can. (Warning: doesn't always work.)

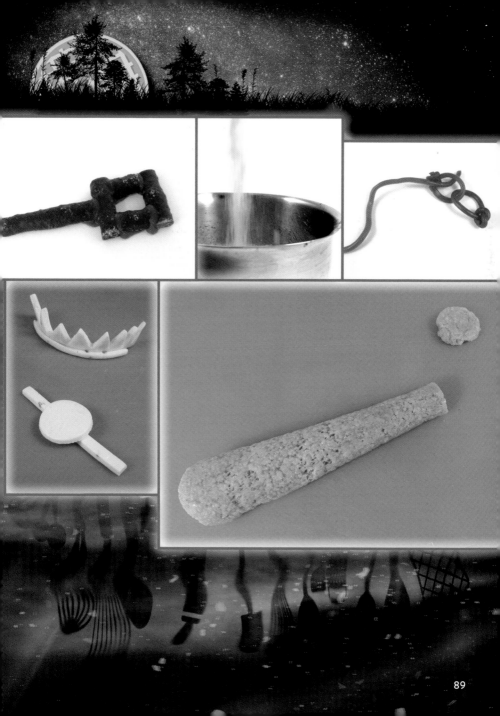

ELEVEN'S EGGOS

DIFFICULTY

So delicious you won't ever want to eat anything else!

INGREDIENTS

Warning: do not steal these ingredients from your local store.

3 ounces dark chocolate
1 Eggo, toasted
1 banana
1 teaspoon strawberry jam
White chocolate buttons

FEEDS

DIRECTIONS

Melt the dark chocolate in a bowl of a pan of simmering water and dip the Eggo in as shown to create the hairline. Leave the Eggo in the fridge to cool.

Use a knife to cut a nose from the banana and affix to the Eggo using a little melted chocolate. Apply a touch of strawberry jam below the nose. Affix the white buttons to the Eggo with melted chocolate and use a paintbrush to dab a bit of chocolate on top of the buttons for the eyes. Drip a little of the melted chocolate onto the Eggo for the mouth. It's time to eat.

Set your treats out on a plate or—for best results—serve them from a box left in the woods.

Mr. Clarke's Plate Set

Featuring Mr Clarke's signature flea-on-tightrope design, this underrated collection is guaranteed to give your dining experience a massive amount of energy.

"There's more than one dimension to my brand…"

1983

MIKE'S ROCK CAKE RESCUE

You're going to fall for this scenic snack

INGREDIENTS

FOR THE CAKE
2 cups all-purpose flour
3 teaspoons baking powder
$\frac{1}{2}$ cup and 1 tablespoon superfine sugar
$\frac{1}{2}$ cup and 1 tablespoon (1 stick and 1 tablespoon)
    unsalted butter, cut into cubes
$\frac{3}{4}$ cup dried fruit
1 large egg
1 tablespoon milk
2 teaspoons vanilla extract or essence
Digestive biscuits
Green, black, and white food coloring
Chocolate twigs
2 packets of blue or green Jell-O

FOR THE BUTTERCREAM FROSTING
2 tablespoons soft butter
$\frac{1}{3}$ cup confectioners' sugar
1 teaspoon milk (if necessary)

FEEDS

DIRECTIONS

TO MAKE THE CAKE

Preheat oven to 350ºF and line two baking trays with baking parchment. Mix the flour, sugar, and baking powder in a bowl and rub in the cubed butter until the mixture looks like breadcrumbs. Then mix in the dried fruit.

In a clean bowl, beat the egg and milk together with the vanilla extract. Add the egg mixture to the dry ingredients and stir with a spoon until the mixture just comes together as a thick, lumpy dough. Divide the mixture into three tiers as shown to make the curved walls of the gorge and place onto the prepared baking trays. Leave space between them as they will flatten and spread out (to double their size) during baking.

Bake the rock cake dough for 15 to 20 minutes, until golden brown. Remove from the oven, allow to cool for a couple of minutes, then turn them out onto a wire rack to cool.

Meanwhile, prepare the Jell-O following the instructions on the packet and pour the mixture into a heavily oiled receptacle (a round pie or tart pan to achieve the shape as shown) before leaving in the fridge to cool. (You want to be able to easily tip it out later.)

TO MAKE THE BUTTERCREAM

Beat the confectioners' sugar and butter together until light and fluffy, adding a little milk if necessary. Add the green food coloring and stir until the correct color is achieved. Fill out a piping bag with nozzle and pipe the buttercream around shortened pieces of chocolate twigs to create the trees and tree trunks.

TO MAKE THE VEGETATION

Crush the biscuits to a fine crumble using a tea towel and rolling pin, or a blender, and add some green food coloring.

TO MAKE THE FIGURE

Roll out some of the pastry and use a sharp knife to create the shape of Mike's body. Using a paintbrush, apply the food coloring. Cake for 10-15 minutes or until the edges begin to turn brown. Use a little melted chocolate to affix the figure to a toothpick and insert into the cake.

FOR THE FINISHING TOUCHES

Tip the Jell-O out of the receptacle and place in between the rock cakes. Decorate as shown with the chocolate trees and biscuit crumble.

Once finished, fall to the floor exhausted and lament how it was you who opened the gate in the first place.

FRIENDS DON'T LI(M)E PIE

DIFFICULTY

A formidable flan that will make your guests flip

INGREDIENTS

1 14-ounce can sweetened condensed
  milk
4 large egg yolks
½ cup fresh lime juice (from about 1
  pound of limes)
1 teaspoon key lime zest, grated
3 tablespoons honey
2 readymade pie crusts
Black, blue, and green food coloring
1 ounce chocolate or edible glue

FEEDS

DIRECTIONS

Go go go go go go go go!

TO MAKE THE PIE

Add the condensed milk, egg yolks, lime juice, and zest to a large bowl and mix thoroughly. Pour into the prepared pie crust, then bake for 15 minutes, or until set. Allow to cool then refrigerate for at least 4 hours, but preferably overnight. When ready, bake for 10-15 minutes or until the edges begin to turn brown.

Roll out the second pie crust and use a sharp knife to create the shapes of the trees, cycles, and van. Using a paintbrush, paint them as shown with food coloring. Place on a baking sheet and bake for 7-10 minutes or until golden brown. To assemble, press the trees and figures into cooked pie surface (use cocktaill sticks for extra stability if necessary). Attach one or two large wooden skewers to the back of the van with a little melted chocolate or edible glue. Pierce the pie dish with the skewers and position the van so it hovers over the figures.

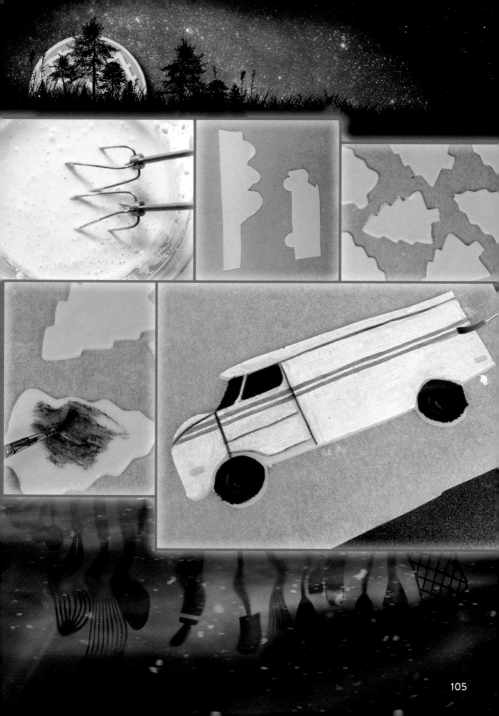

THE UPSIDE DOWN CAKE

DIFFICULTY

Cross over to the other side with this inter-dimensional delight

INGREDIENTS

FOR THE CAKE
1 1/3 cups (2 2/3 sticks) butter
2 cups sugar
6 eggs (lightly beaten)
3 cups and 2 tablespoons all-purpose flour
6 teaspoons baking powder
Just under 1 cup cocoa powder, sieved
3 to 4 tablespoons milk

FOR THE BUTTERCREAM FROSTING
1/2 cup and 1 tablespoon (1 stick and 1 tablespoon) soft butter
Just under 2 cups confectioners' sugar
1 to 2 tablespoons milk
Blue and black food coloring
1 pound white fondant
3 1/2 ounces black fondant

TO DECORATE
2 ounces dark chocolate
1 chocolate egg
Yellow food color spray
1 packet chocolate twigs

You will need:
A piping bag with a small regular-shaped nozzle
Four cake stands to support the cake at each corner
A hazmat suit

FEEDS

DIRECTIONS

You will need to find your nearest portal. We used the one at Hawkins National but it's worth looking in tree trunks.

FOR THE CAKE

Preheat the oven to 350°F. Grease and line a 13 x 9-inch deep rectangular baking pan. Cream the butter and sugar until pale in color, light and fluffy. Add the eggs very gradually, beating well between each addition. Combine the flour and cocoa powder, then fold into the mix until blended. Add enough milk to give a dropping consistency and spoon into the prepared pan, smoothing the top and making a slight dip in the center. Bake for 45 to 55 minutes, or until firm to the touch and a knife inserted in the center comes out clean. Cool in the pan for a few minutes, then turn out onto a rack to cool completely.

Don't be distracted by Barb's corpse.

TO MAKE THE BUTTERCREAM FROSTING

Beat the butter in a large bowl until soft. Gently add half the confectioners' sugar and beat until smooth. Add the remaining confectioners' sugar with a little milk, adding more as necessary to make a light fluffy icing. Add the blue and black food coloring little by little, and mix until well combined. Then use a palette knife to apply the frosting to the surface of the cake.

TO MAKE THE TREES

Place the chocolate in a heatproof bowl and set over a pan of simmering water, stirring occasionally just until melted. Remove from the heat and allow to cool a little before spooning into a piping bag. Pipe the trees onto a piece of baking parchment and leave to cool. Carefully affix the trees to the cake's frosting.

TO MAKE THE EGG

Use a sharp knife to cut the top from the egg, rough up the edges, and use the yellow food spray to color before fixing it to the frosting.

TO MAKE THE OTHER SIDE OF THE CAKE (THE UPSIDE DOWN)

Roll out the white fondant and the black fondant. Drape first the black fondant where the hole in the wall will be, and then overlay with the white fondant across the whole of the cake. Use a sharp knife to cut the white fondant away as desired and then decorate using a piping bag and melted chocolate as show. Use the yellow spray to color the chocolate sticks to create the rails. Spray a thin rope of the white fondant yellow and overlay with small pieces of the black fondant as shown for the caution strip.

TO MAKE THE FIGURES

Use the remaining fondant with food coloring to decorate using a paintbrush where necessary.

Carefully remove any wormlike creatures from your guests' airways and dispatch them with a few well-aimed rounds.

WILL'S
SLUG SURPRISE

A meal so good you're going to want to bring it up, again and again

20 ounces white chocolate
10 ounces pink chocolate
1 packet of strawberry or raspberry
  Jell-O
7 tablespoons soft butter
$1\frac{1}{3}$ cups confectioners' sugar, sieved
White chocolate buttons
Black food coloring
1 packet of gummy worms

You will need:
A thick paintbrush
Some party balloons

FEEDS

DIRECTIONS

Don't forget to wash your hands before dinner. Inflate a balloon to the eventual size of your chocolate head. Melt the chocolate in a bowl over a pan of simmering water. Set the chocolate aside to cool for a moment before using the brush to paint a layer on the balloon. Leave the chocolate on the balloon to set before repeating the method until you have made a thick chocolate shell all around the balloon, except at the knot.

In the meantime, dispose of any excess slugs down the sinkhole.

Use a sharp knife to pop and then remove the balloon. Leave the chocolate shell in the fridge to harden. Then follow the instructions on the packet of jelly and leave in the fridge to set. Melt the dark chocolate in a bowl over a simmering pan of water and use the piping bag to pipe on the hair. Use a little of the melted chocolate to apply the white chocolate buttons and use a paintbrush to apply the black food coloring for the eyes.

Use a paintbrush to decorate the gummy worm with food coloring. With a knife, carefully cut a hole in the chocolate shell for the mouth and spoon in some of the Jell-O, followed by painted gummy worm.

Now take your seat at the table in the knowledge that you haven't truly escaped the Upside Down . . . Try to enjoy your Christmas dinner, though.

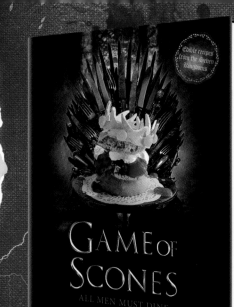

Great recipes. No meth-in around.

Ba king Ba d

99.1% PURE 100% EDIBLE

WALTER WHEAT

Edible recipes from the Seven Kingdoms

GAME OF SCONES

ALL MEN MUST DINE
(A Parody)

JAMMY LANNISTER

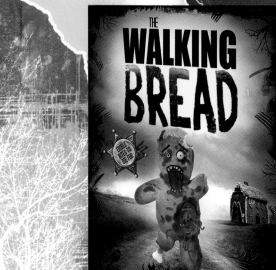

THE
WALKING BREAD

EDIBLE BITES TO DIE FOR

RICK GRAINS

FOREWORD BY MARY BURIED

FOLLOW US

Facebook
@strangerfillings

Instagram
@themuffinbrothers

Twitter
@strangerfilling

Author's Note

This book is a loving tribute from a fan and not intended to lay claim to the genius creations of the TV show on which it comments. I love *Stranger Things* and I love to bake. The real aim of this book is to use baking as a medium by which I am reviewing the show; to look back on the first season and—with eggs, flour, sugar, water, and some food coloring—making a unique comment on it.

In this book, the dreaded Demogorgon becomes a delectable treat— just as Nancy and Jonathan prepare to take to the Upside Down and save Will, you can take on the monster by nibbling off his arms and legs. The essence of Hopper—coffee and booze—is translated into a tasty cupcake that proves there's an ooey gooey center under that gruff exterior. Barb's fateful "dip" in the pool becomes a literal dip you can eat in the company of friends who would never leave you behind. Food is a language in *Stranger Fillings*, one I hope we can use to delve deeper into the themes of this brilliant show.

I hope fans will read this book and enjoy reliving moments from the show as they follow the recipes. Who knows, it might even add a new dimension to things!

Bon appetit!

The Author

WITH THANKS TO...

Anna Valentine

Emma Smith

Mark McGinlay

and all of the team at Trapeze

ABOUT THE AUTHORS

The Muffin Brothers are level 14 Dungeons & Dragons wizards, ham radio enthusiasts, and two of the best bakers the 1980s ever saw.

This book was written in conjunction with their mother, using a system of blinking lights.

They divide their time between Indiana and the Upside Down.